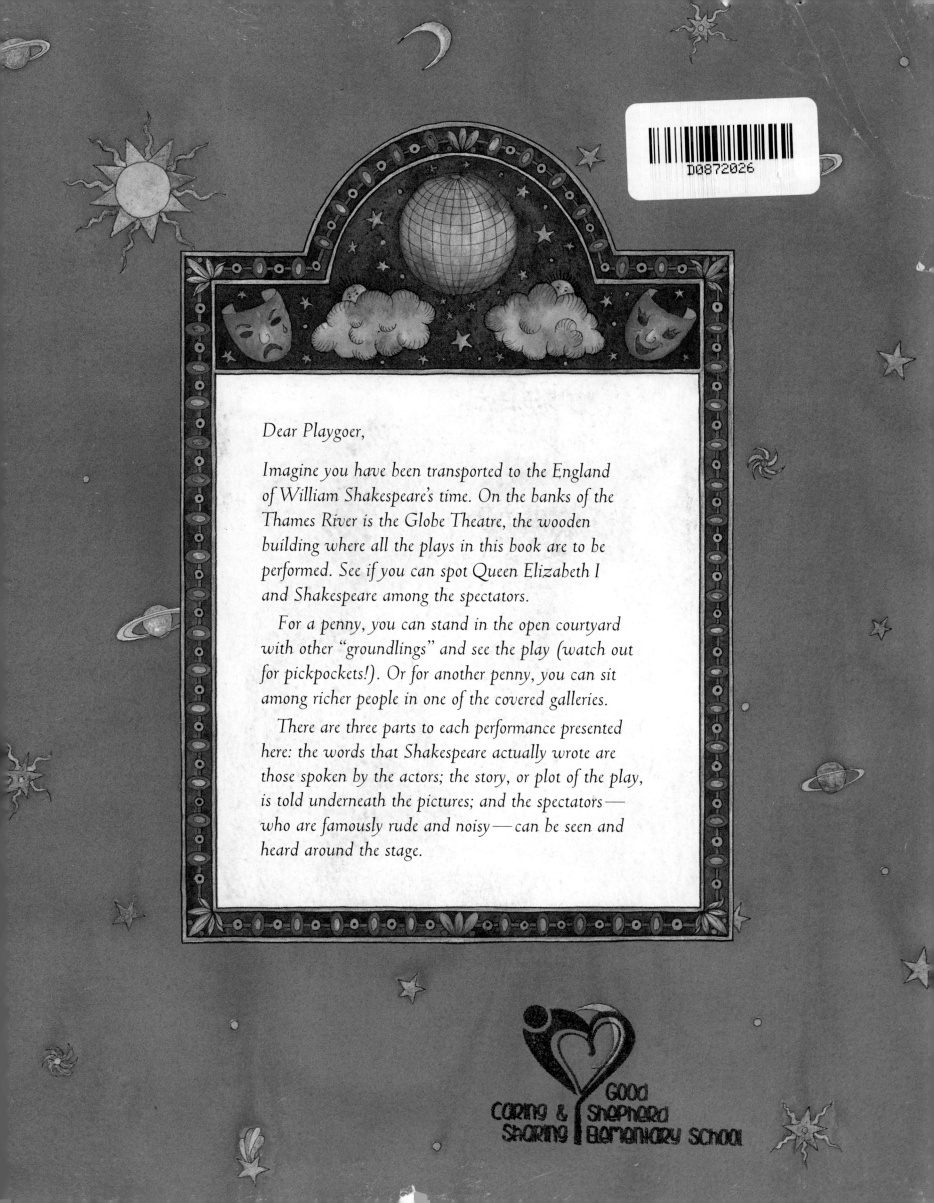

Dear Playgoer,

Imagine you have been transported to the England
of William Shakespeare's time. On the banks of the
Thames River is the Globe Theatre, the wooden
building where all the plays in this book are to be
performed. See if you can spot Queen Elizabeth I
and Shakespeare among the spectators.

For a penny, you can stand in the open courtyard
with other "groundlings" and see the play (watch out
for pickpockets!). Or for another penny, you can sit
among richer people in one of the covered galleries.

There are three parts to each performance presented
here: the words that Shakespeare actually wrote are
those spoken by the actors; the story, or plot of the play,
is told underneath the pictures; and the spectators—
who are famously rude and noisy—can be seen and
heard around the stage.

First U.S. edition 1998

Library of Congress Cataloging-in-Publication Data
Williams, Marcia.
Tales from Shakespeare : seven plays / presented and illustrated by Marcia Williams. — 1st U.S. ed.
p.   cm.
Summary: Retells seven of Shakespeare's plays—Romeo and Juliet, Hamlet, A Midsummer Night's Dream,
Macbeth, The Winter's Tale, Julius Caesar, and The Tempest—in comic-book format.
ISBN 0-7636-0441-0
[1. Shakespeare, William, 1564–1616—Adaptations.   2. Cartoons and comics.]   1. Title.
PN6727.W475T35   1998
741.5'973—dc21   97-42165

2 4 6 8 10 9 7 5 3

Printed in Belgium

This book was typeset in Monotype Centaur and Truesdell.
The illustrations were done in watercolor and ink.

Candlewick Press
2067 Massachusetts Avenue
Cambridge, Massachusetts 02140

visit us at www.candlewick.com

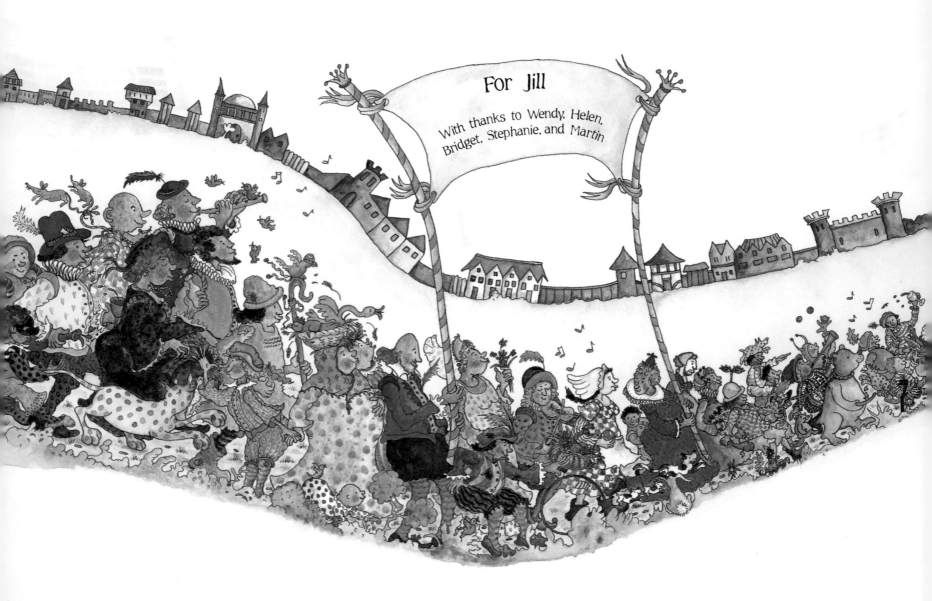

For Jill

With thanks to Wendy, Helen,
Bridget, Stephanie, and Martin

Tales from
SHAKESPEARE

SEVEN PLAYS PRESENTED
AND ILLUSTRATED BY

Marcia Williams

CANDLEWICK PRESS
CAMBRIDGE, MASSACHUSETTS

ROMEO and JULIET

MONTAGUES

CAPULETS

Go, sirrah, trudge about
Through fair Verona; find
those persons out
Whose names are written there,
and to them say,
My house and welcome on
their pleasure stay.

I am sent to find those persons
Whose names are here writ. . .
I must to the learned.

Do you bite your
thumb at us, sir?

In the ancient Italian city of Verona, Lord Capulet was planning a party. He was sure no members of the Montague family would turn up, as the Capulets and Montagues had been feuding for years. The quarrel ran so deep that even their servants fought. But Lord Capulet was wrong.

Is love a tender thing? It is too rough,
Too rude, too boisterous; and it pricks like thorn.

Did my heart love
till now?

Romeo, Lord Montague's son, and Mercutio, his friend, *did* come—in disguise. Romeo was infatuated with Lord Capulet's niece, Rosaline.

However, Romeo forgot all about Rosaline when he saw Lord Capulet's sweet young daughter, Juliet. Her beauty stole his heart.

Uncle, this is
a Montague!

Young Romeo, is it?

O! She doth
teach the
torches to burn
bright.

'Tis a
shame.

He shall be endur'd.

A snowy dove
trooping with crows.

The only
son of your
great enemy.

My only love
sprung from my
only hate!

Nuts
for sale!
Eat my
fine
nuts!

And
her
only 13.

Unfortunately, Romeo was recognized by Lord Capulet's fiery nephew, Tybalt.

But Lord Capulet forbade fighting at his ball and made Romeo welcome.

So Romeo wooed Juliet and soon their love was mutual, despite the feud.

Will you
be my
Juliet?

No!

He loves her.

Go on!
Kiss her.

O Romeo, Romeo.

As the party ended, Juliet ran to her balcony to declare her love for Romeo to the stars.

O gentle Romeo.

O! It is my love.

Romeo risked death by climbing the Capulets' orchard wall to see Juliet.

'Tis but thy name that is my enemy.

That night, the loving pair agreed to wed in secret, lest their feuding families part them.

Madam! *Parting is such a sweet sorrow.*

Hence will I go to my ghostly father's cell.

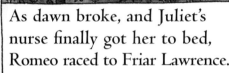

As dawn broke, and Juliet's nurse finally got her to bed, Romeo raced to Friar Lawrence.

Wast thou with Rosaline?

Rosaline, I have forgot that name.

The friar agreed to marry the sweethearts, hoping this would unite the families.

These violent delights have violent ends.

Later that morning, Juliet joined Romeo at the chapel, and the happy pair were wed.

Ah! Juliet! *True love.*

Violent ends.

Then Romeo and Juliet parted, as they knew they must, until Friar Lawrence had broken the news to their families.

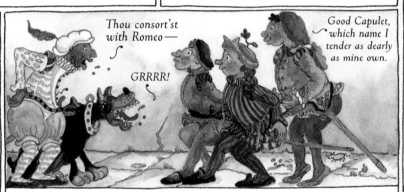

Thou consort'st with Romeo— *Good Capulet, which name I tender as dearly as mine own.*

GRRRR!

On the way home, Romeo met his good friends Benvolio and Mercutio, who were being harangued by Tybalt for consorting with a Montague.

Put thy rapier up.

Romeo, now related to Tybalt by his marriage, tried to prevent a fight, but failed.

A plague o' both your houses! They have made worms' meat of me.

Tybalt and Mercutio's swords clashed and Mercutio fell dead.

Romeo, away! Be gone! . . . Tybalt's slain. *O! I am Fortune's fool.*

Provoked by his friend's death, Romeo struck Tybalt a fatal blow.

Buzz off.

Soppy nonsense!

Yes, dear.

Watch, dear. Nice Mr. Shakespeare wrote this just for you.

Boring.

Well done, boys, nice deaths.

Juliet was carried to the family burial vault, from where, according to the friar's plan, Romeo would rescue her.

But the friar's letter, telling Romeo of the scheme, went astray. A messenger told Romeo the false news of Juliet's sudden "death."

Romeo bought poison and went to the tomb. There he found Paris, who in his misery attacked Romeo, who slew him in defense.

Then Romeo gave Juliet a kiss and drank the poison. Just too late, Friar Lawrence arrived, now aware that his letter had not reached Romeo.

As the friar cried out in horror, Juliet awoke to see Romeo, lifeless beside her.

Hearing voices approach, the friar fled. But Juliet, unable to imagine life without Romeo, took up his dagger and, stabbing herself, fell dead upon her husband's body.

When the families of the Montagues and Capulets arrived upon this tragic scene, they were grief stricken at the consequences of their vendetta. Lord Capulet and Lord Montague vowed to raise a golden statue to each other's child. Thus they buried their feud, along with their precious children, Romeo and his sweet Juliet.

HAMLET
Prince of Denmark

As Hamlet, prince of Denmark, kept watch with his friend Horatio on the battlements of Elsinore Castle, his father's ghost appeared to him. The ghost told Hamlet that he had been murdered by his brother, Claudius, and urged Hamlet to take revenge.

Gentle Hamlet had idolized his father and was outraged when his mother, Queen Gertrude, married his uncle, Claudius, who then became king. But Hamlet had not suspected his uncle of murder.

Hamlet kept the ghost's secret, but all at court, including the king's chamberlain, Polonius, noticed how unstable Hamlet had become.

He often exaggerated his madness so that his uncle, Claudius, and Polonius would not realize that he was suspicious.

Even Ophelia, Polonius's daughter, suffered from Hamlet's erratic behavior. Hamlet's feelings for her fluctuated between tenderness and scorn.

Unable to trust anyone at court, Hamlet felt miserable and confused. Should he take his own life or that of his father's murderer, Claudius?

Hamlet's mother, unaware that Claudius had murdered Hamlet's father, thought his madness was grief for the good king's death.

Polonius was sure that Hamlet's madness stemmed from his love for Ophelia. Only Claudius feared a more sinister reason.

Meanwhile, Hamlet's distress grew daily as he watched his mother, so recently widowed, and his murderous uncle together. Yet he hesitated to take revenge without more evidence. Then the arrival of an acting troupe gave Hamlet an idea of how to unmask King Claudius.

Before the assembled court, the actors, on Hamlet's orders, put on a play mimicking the ghost's story of his murder and its consequences. Claudius was so affected by the murder scene that he rushed from the room; Hamlet no longer doubted his uncle's guilt.

Claudius realized that he had been discovered and, hoping to learn more, encouraged Polonius to spy on Hamlet and Queen Gertrude.

From behind the drapes, Polonius overheard Hamlet grow violent when his mother spoke of Claudius as his "father." He cried out in alarm.

Hamlet, thinking it was Claudius's voice, plunged his sword through the drapes, killing Polonius. Anger made Hamlet unrepentant.

Hamlet continued to chide his mother until his father's ghost appeared, urging him to be gentler, but to avenge his death.

Polonius's death gave Claudius an excuse to be rid of Hamlet. Claudius sent the prince to England with two of his spies, who carried a letter ordering the English to execute Hamlet upon arrival. But Hamlet found the letter and exchanged the spies' names for his own.

On the journey, their ship was attacked by pirates. Hamlet leaped aboard to fight, while his companions fled to England—and their deaths.

The pirates, discovering that they had Prince Hamlet on board, returned him safely to Denmark, hoping for future favors.

At Elsinore, Hamlet was greeted with the news of Ophelia's death. Deranged by her father's violent end, Ophelia had been garlanding a willow tree when she fell into the brook below and drowned. Hamlet was heartbroken. So too was Laertes, who mourned her loss as only a brother can.

In fact, Laertes blamed Hamlet for killing both his father and his sister, and he longed for Hamlet's death as much as Claudius did. The pair therefore plotted to kill Hamlet and make his death look like an accident. To do this they issued a challenge to the prince.

Hamlet was tempted into a fencing match with Laertes, who fought with a poisoned sword instead of a blunt foil. When Laertes drew blood, Hamlet let fly his fury, and in the scuffle, the swords changed hands. Then Laertes too was wounded by his own deadly weapon.

Just then, the queen cried out. Unwittingly, she had drunk from a poisoned cup, prepared for Hamlet by Claudius, in case Laertes failed to kill him. Queen Gertrude collapsed on the floor. Hamlet at once suspected his treacherous uncle.

As Laertes lay dying, he told Hamlet that they had both been mortally wounded, and he confessed his part in Claudius's plot.

Reacting to his uncle's fresh villainy, Hamlet stabbed Claudius with the lethal sword, then forced him to drink from the cup of poison.

At last Hamlet had avenged his father's and now his mother's murder. As death drew near, he saw Horatio reach for the poison.

Horatio wished to join his friend in death. But Hamlet persuaded him that he must live to tell the true story of Prince Hamlet.

This Horatio did when, moments later, the prince of Norway arrived. After hearing the story, the prince ordered his canons to fire a salute. For all who heard the tale knew that, had the fates allowed, Hamlet, prince of Denmark, would have been a most royal and noble king.

A Midsummer Night's Dream

Long ago, in Athens, the law decreed that a daughter must marry the man of her father's choice or be punished. Consequently, Egeus had brought his daughter, Hermia, to the court of Theseus, duke of Athens, for refusing Demetrius, the man of his choice. Hermia actually loved Lysander.

Theseus was sympathetic and gave Hermia four days to choose between love and duty.

Unable to part, Lysander and Hermia told their friend Helena they would flee Athens.

So, that very night, they fled to the woods, away from the city and its cruel law.

Meanwhile, Helena revealed their plans to Demetrius because she loved him, and he had once loved her. But Demetrius was now obsessed with Hermia and set out after the runaway lovers, followed by the lovelorn Helena.

Not Hermia, but Helena I love.

Do not say so.

To honor Helen, and to be her knight!

Wherefore was I to this keen mockery born?

I swoon almost with fear.

So, by the flower's magic, Lysander forgot his love for Hermia and fell instantly in love with Helena.

Shocked by Lysander's unexpected love, Helena ran off, pursued by Lysander.

Thus, poor Hermia woke alone. Fearfully, she set out in search of Lysander.

Which is the proper play?

Are we all met?

Pat, pat; and here's a marvellous convenient place for our rehearsal.

All this while Titania slept on, unaware that the troupe of Athenians, led by Bottom and Peter Quince, had chosen to rehearse their play nearby. It was a perfect opportunity for the mischievous Puck to play one of his tricks, for Titania's eyelids still glistened with magic juice.

If I were, fair Thisby, I were only thine.

Yoo-hoo! Puck.

Has he got fleas?

Suddenly, at the height of the action, Bottom, the weaver, appeared wearing a donkey's head! The other actors fled in fright. Then Puck, who had transformed Bottom into this ridiculous creature, guided him to the sleeping Titania's side.

Get her jewels next.

Sssh! I'm listening.

How do they do that?

Can we do that to Daddy?

I need to wee!

When Titania awoke, the first creature she saw was Bottom, with a donkey's head! Instantly, she fell in love with him. Bottom was not displeased by the attention, especially when Titania ordered her fairies to attend his every whim.

As Puck reported all this to Oberon, Hermia hurried past. Demetrius was close behind, but now, exhausted and disheartened, he paused to rest. Realizing Puck's error, Oberon sent him to fetch Helena, while he anointed Demetrius's lids with the flower juice.

So when Demetrius awoke and saw Helena, he loved her once again. Helena, far from being happy about this, believed herself mocked.

When Hermia arrived she quickly understood that both Lysander *and* Demetrius now loved Helena. Hermia screamed insults at Helena.

Puck, on Oberon's orders, drew the lovers on and on until, tired and confused, they fell asleep.

Then Puck anointed Lysander's eyelids in order to restore his love for Hermia.

As Bottom lay sleeping in Titania's arms, Oberon put an antidote on her lids.

Then Oberon woke Titania, who was so mortified at being seen with a snoring donkey that she promised Oberon the changeling boy.

Oberon, satisfied at last, danced happily away with Titania, leaving Puck to restore Bottom to his usual self.

My love shall hear the music of my hounds.

I beg the law!

As day dawned, a hunting party entered the woods, led by Duke Theseus and Hippolyta; Egeus was also in the party.

When they happened upon the reunited lovers, Egeus was still eager to impose the law of Athens on his daughter, Hermia.

Are we the audience or are they?

Well roared, lion.

Well shone, moon.

ROAR!

O sweet and lovely wall. Show me thy chink.

Did you pay for two plays?

RESERVED

But it was Theseus's wedding day, and when he saw the young people back with their original loved ones, he overruled Egeus. He bade the party return to Athens and resolved to have all three couples wed that very day: himself to Hippolyta, Hermia to Lysander, and Helena to Demetrius. After the ceremony, Bottom and his troupe were called to put on their play, which earned them all a goodly sum and much applause. Then the whole company, at last restored to happy harmony, retired to bed.

Hand in hand, with fairy grace, Will we sing, and bless this place.

IF WE SHADOWS HAVE OFFENDED, THINK BUT THIS, AND ALL IS MENDED. THAT YOU HAVE BUT SLUMBER'D HERE, WHILE THESE VISIONS DID APPEAR.

Ooh! That's so pretty.

Slumber? With all that going on?

That left the way clear for the fairy king and queen, attended by Puck, to bless the palace of Theseus and bid all good night—the perfect end to the story, or to a beautifully woven midsummer night's dream in the enchanted woods.

SOLD OUT

Are they all happy now?

We've got fairies in our house!

Most people call them fleas!

Well, that's what I call a finale!

MACBETH

Macbeth and Banquo, two Scottish generals living under the reign of King Duncan, were returning home to Inverness across a barren heath. They had just bravely defeated an army of rebels, much to the delight of the king, who was also Macbeth's cousin.

Suddenly, as if from nowhere, three hideous witches appeared. The first witch greeted Macbeth as Thane (or Lord) of Glamis, which was his correct title. The second greeted him as Thane of Cawdor, which he was not, and the third as King of Scotland, an honor held by Duncan.

Just before the witches vanished they also prophesied that Banquo would never be king, but that he would father kings.

As the two generals stood, stunned, news arrived that the king had made Macbeth Thane of Cawdor, in honor of his victory.

Stop your croak!

Hail, king that shalt be!

... look like the innocent flower,
But be the serpent under't.

Shoo!

The witches' first prediction had come true! Macbeth sent word to his ambitious wife. Would he, they wondered, soon be king?

When Macbeth reached his castle, Lady Macbeth, her mind already fixed on the crown, was plotting King Duncan's death.

You see, you too could act!

See, see, our honor'd hostess!

... honors deep and broad wherewith Your majesty loads our house.

Typical, says one thing, means another.

King Duncan duly arrived with his two sons: Prince Malcolm, heir to the throne, and Donalbain. They had come to thank Macbeth for his valor in battle. Lady Macbeth played the charming hostess, but secretly urged her husband to kill the king that very night.

Does she want to be king?

I have drugg'd their possets.

Is this a dagger which I see before me, The handle toward my hand?

That which hath made them drunk hath made me bold.

She's more wicked than the witches.

In preparation for the evil deed, Lady Macbeth drugged King Duncan's two guards.

Macbeth, agonizing over the murder, saw a phantom dagger hovering before him.

Fearing her husband would fail, Lady Macbeth crept into Duncan's room herself.

You see, she's all heart, really.

Had he not resembled my father as he slept, I had done't.

Screw your courage to the sticking place!

I have done the deed.

One death always leads to another.

But the sleeping king looked so like her own father that she was unable to kill him.

Lady Macbeth summoned her husband, pouring scorn on his own hesitation.

So, reluctantly, Macbeth took the daggers from the drugged guards and slew the king.

Shall we throw apple cores at them?

No, I want to see what happens.

I don't think this is quite suitable for children.

He'll have to kill the sons next.

With their daggers bloodied, the grooms were blamed. Macbeth, claiming vengeance, killed them both to safeguard his secret.

Despite their display of grief, many suspected the Macbeths of the murder. The king's sons, fearing for their own lives, fled Scotland.

Macbeth, as next in line to the throne, was then crowned king, fulfilling the third prophecy.

Haunted by guilt, but still anxious to retain power, Macbeth worried that Banquo's descendants, not his own, would one day reign, as had also been foretold.

So Macbeth resolved to murder Banquo and his son, Fleance, and thus invited all the local thanes to a feast. As Banquo and Fleance made their way to the palace, they were brutally attacked by Macbeth's hired assassins. Fleance managed to escape, but Banquo died.

Oblivious to this horrific deed, the other thanes were merrily dining when Banquo's ghost suddenly appeared. Only Macbeth could see the specter and it so unnerved him that the queen soon dismissed their guests, lest they wonder at the strange behavior of their king.

Thereafter, Macbeth and his queen began to suffer long, sleepless nights filled with hideous dreams. Yet Macbeth was still obsessed with not losing the throne, so he returned to the heath to seek out the witches. He found them in a cave, chanting over a cauldron of boiling hell-broth, from which three apparitions rose: the first was an armed head, which warned Macbeth to beware of Macduff, the thane of Fife; the second was a bloody child, who told Macbeth that no man born of woman could harm him; the third was another child, wearing a crown and holding a tree, who reassured Macbeth that he would never be vanquished until Great Birnam Wood came to Dunsinane Hill, where Macbeth's castle stood.

When Macbeth asked if Banquo's heirs would reign, the cauldron sank into the ground and eight ghostly kings passed by, followed by Banquo's ghost. The last king carried a mirror that showed many kings, and Macbeth knew them to be Banquo's descendants.

From this day, insecurity plagued Macbeth. So when he heard that Macduff, thane of Fife, had joined forces with Prince Malcolm, Macbeth ordered the death of Macduff's wife and children. This bloody deed lost Macbeth many friends and determined Malcolm and Macduff to seek revenge.

Then Macbeth received a terrible blow: his queen, who had never come to terms with her guilt and whose nights and days were ceaselessly haunted by ghastly visions, finally succumbed to death. Macbeth felt totally alone. Still more grave news followed. . . .

Thousands of Prince Malcolm's troops were fast approaching, shielded behind branches cut from Great Birnam Wood. Thus it appeared that the forest moved toward Dunsinane Hill and Macbeth's castle, the event predicted to precede Macbeth's downfall.

Macbeth still believed himself invulnerable. Rallying his remaining forces, he waged a bloody war, until he met Macduff, face to face. When Macduff disclosed that he had not been born by natural means, but by cesarean birth with the help of a surgeon, Macbeth knew his end had come.

Now Prince Malcolm, the rightful heir, claimed his father's throne. Macbeth was dead and the people rejoiced. The wicked reign of Macbeth and his ambitious queen had ended just as had been prophesied. Scotland was at peace, ruled once more by a true and noble king.

The Winter's Tale

One winter, King Leontes of Sicily, Queen Hermione, and their young son, Mamillius, were contentedly awaiting the birth of a second child. Polixenes, king of Bohemia, had come to visit and was now about to depart, much against Leontes's wishes.

But Hermione succeeded where her husband had failed and persuaded Polixenes to stay longer with them.

Instead of pleasing Leontes, this made him insanely jealous. He thought that Hermione and Polixenes must be in love.

King Leontes told Camillo, his advisor, of his belief, wishing him to poison Polixenes.

Unable to change Leontes's mind, Camillo fled with Polixenes to Bohemia.

Meanwhile, Mamillius related a sad tale to distract his mother from the king's anger.

Meanwhile, a storm drove the ship carrying Perdita onto the shores of Bohemia. Perdita, with a bundle of keepsakes, was saved, but the ship and all its crew were lost.

Luckily, Perdita was found by a shepherd, who cared for her as a daughter for fifteen years.

Perdita was so delightful that Prince Florizel, son of King Polixenes, fell in love with her.

All this time, Camillo was also in Bohemia but unaware of Perdita. Polixenes was angry that his son was courting a shepherdess and asked Camillo to visit her.

Well disguised, Polixenes and Camillo met Florizel and Perdita and were innocently asked to witness their engagement.

Polixenes suddenly threw off his disguise. He forbade his son to marry a shepherdess and he ordered Florizel to return to court.

But Camillo, charmed by the pair, persuaded them to escape to Sicily and beg King Leontes's help, while he sought Polixenes's approval.

King Leontes welcomed Polixenes's son. Alas, Perdita's striking likeness to Hermione brought sad memories flooding back.

As King Leontes talked of the past, it dawned on the shepherd, who had escorted the pair, that Perdita could be Leontes's daughter. Many rumors flew about as to how this was proven, but it *was* proven and the king was beside himself with happiness.

Leontes took his daughter to see a statue of her mother, Hermione, rumored to be kept by Paulina. In spite of the welcome arrival of Polixenes and Camillo, Leontes could not take his eyes off the lifelike statue.

Then Paulina called for music, and to everyone's amazement, the statue began to move. Hermione descended the pedestal. The time had come for the queen to be reunited with her family and friends.

King Polixenes, discovering his son's shepherdess to be a princess, gave his blessing for Florizel and Perdita's marriage, joining the two families in harmony once more. King Leontes gave Paulina's hand in marriage to Camillo, for they held each other in deep affection. Thus ended the strange story of how Paulina had kept Hermione hidden and how Perdita had been found—a wonderful winter's tale to tell by the fireside.

It was a day of celebration and the streets of ancient Rome swarmed with citizens cheering Julius Caesar's victory over his rival, Pompey. At that time, Rome was a Republic—ruled by the people through their senators. Now some politicians feared that Caesar would want to rule Rome himself.

As Caesar paraded to the games, a soothsayer warned him to beware the Ides of March, or the fifteenth day of the month. Caesar scoffed.

Two senators, Brutus and Cassius, watched Caesar's triumphant expression. They supported the Republic and feared Caesar's ambition.

On his return from the games, Caesar did not look so pleased. Casca, a friend of the two senators, explained what had happened:

Caesar's supporter, Mark Antony, had offered him the crown. To Caesar's dismay, when he hesitantly refused it, the crowd roared its approval.

In raising money for their armies, Brutus and Cassius quarreled violently. Their friendship and the battle for Rome seemed doomed.

But suddenly Brutus's temper cooled. He confessed that grief had overwhelmed him: his beloved wife, Portia, had killed herself.

As Cassius comforted Brutus, news arrived: Antony and Octavius, having executed many Republican senators, were marching to Phillipi.

The remaining conspirators unwisely agreed to set out for Phillipi and confront their enemies, just as Antony hoped they would.

Drums rolled as dawn broke and the battle for Rome began. All day it raged. But, weakened by the long march to Phillipi, Brutus and Cassius's armies were no match for the enemy. By evening the conspirators had been defeated. Those who had not died in battle fell upon their own swords, rather than witness the fall of the Roman Republic. Octavius was impatient to celebrate their victory, but Antony paused to pay his respects to Brutus, whom he knew had been motivated by neither greed nor envy, only by his love for Rome and its people.

THE TEMPEST

Many years ago on a mystical isle, young Miranda and her loving father, Prospero, watched as a ship foundered in a fierce and terrible tempest. Prospero had been preparing for this moment for years, developing his magic powers from a rare book until he could control the elements. Miranda suspected that her father had caused the storm, but had no idea why such a gentle man should wish to harm anyone. So Prospero revealed how he and his daughter had been cast away on the island, twelve years before.

For then thou wast not out three years old.

Thy father was the duke of Milan.

Me, poor man, my library was dukedom large enough.

My brother, and thy uncle, call'd Antonio . . .

did believe he was indeed the duke.

The king of Naples . . . hearkens my brother's suit.

They hurried us aboard a barque;

bore us some leagues to sea.

Some food we had, and some fresh water.

Here in this island we arrived.

Prospero had been duke of Milan until his brother, Antonio, aided by Alonso, king of Naples, seized power. Prospero and Miranda were set adrift in a tiny boat, but luckily a friend, Gonzalo, had secreted books and provisions on board. These sustained the pair until they drifted onto an island.

The only inhabitants on this isle were the monster Caliban and the sprites his mother had trapped in trees before she died. Caliban became Prospero's servant, as did Ariel, an airy sprite. Ariel, who was invisible to all but Prospero, had been freed from a tree by Prospero's magic and in return had promised to serve him faithfully for twelve years.

As the wise old bear once said, you're never too young for adventure.

We like this already.

I bet he picks his nose.

When I was little, sprites were two for a ducat!

Give us a posy.

Can you see Ariel?

No.

I think Ariel's hidden in the star.

You don't know nothing.

He's right.

Who's right?

I'm right. Ariel's just air.

Know-it-all.

By accident most strange, bountiful fortune, Now my dear lady, hath mine enemies Brought to this shore.

Prospero told Miranda that the storm-tossed ship carried his old enemies. Then, seeing Ariel approach, Prospero put a plan into action and sent Miranda to sleep.

But are they, Ariel, safe?

Not a hair perish'd. The king's son have I landed by himself.

Ariel spirited the ship's company ashore, isolating all but Antonio, Gonzalo, and King Alonso. So the king feared that his son, Prince Ferdinand, must have drowned.

The thunder's over now, dearie.

Go, make thyself like to a nymph of the sea.

Ariel, now in the guise of a sea nymph, went to fetch Ferdinand to Prospero's cave.

Hag-seed, hence! Fetch us in fuel.

I must obey: his art is of such power.

Having dispatched Caliban to gather wood, Prospero then woke Miranda.

I might call him A thing divine.

O you wonder!

Full fathom five thy father lies.

Drawn to the cave by Ariel's singing, Ferdinand stared in wonder at lovely Miranda.

Potato?

. . . and hast put thyself upon this island as a spy.

No, as I am a man.

There's nothing ill can dwell in such a temple.

The two youngsters fell in love, as Prospero had planned. Adversity, he hoped, would seal the bond, so he accused Ferdinand of spying.

I'll manacle thy neck and feet together.

Beseech you, father!

He forbade Miranda to talk to Ferdinand and sent him to shift logs, which Ferdinand did willingly, to stay close to his beloved.

A little adversity does wonders for love.

Miranda, there are other men in the world.

I'll bear your logs the while.

No, precious creature.

For hours, Ferdinand hauled logs. Miranda never left his side.

Take my daughter.

Prospero watched Miranda and Ferdinand's love blossom, and finally he relented.

He conjured up a flock of nymphs to sing a blessing on their engagement.

PRIVATE BOX KEEP OUT

It's a sprite.

Lo now! Lo! I'll fall flat.

Meanwhile, Caliban gathered driftwood, until a looming figure made him hide under his cloak.

Alas! The storm is come again.

It was Trinculo, King Alonso's jester, who, fearing a storm, also crawled under the cloak.

This is some monster of the isle.

Minutes later, Stefano, the king's drunken butler, fell over the heaving bundle.

You're right there, you drunkard!

Jug!

If they've been shipwrecked, why aren't they wet?

It's magic, stupids.

I think I can see Ariel.

Only Prospero can.

Trinculo and Stefano were delighted to be reunited. Caliban, unaware of the shipwreck, thought they had dropped from the moon.

Thinking they must be very powerful, Caliban urged the pair to assassinate Prospero. Ariel overheard and flew off to tell his master.

When the traitor Caliban drew near with his companions, Prospero was ready. Ariel had strewn Prospero's finest clothes before the cave.

Caliban, Trinculo, and Stefano crept up, ready to kill Prospero, but were distracted by the array of handsome garments.

When the murderous trio were half dressed, Prospero unleashed a pack of snarling phantom hounds. Driven by Ariel, the dogs chased the rascals far off across the island. Then Ariel returned to aid Prospero: the time had come for him to settle the score with his brother and King Alonso.

King Alonso, Antonio, and the good Gonzalo had been vainly searching for Ferdinand.

Tired and hungry, they were in despair, but then a table of food suddenly materialized.

Amazed, they were about to eat when Ariel, disguised as a harpy, made the food vanish.

Ariel reminded them of their sins against Prospero. Guilt and fear froze their spirits.

Ariel drew them into a magic circle, where they were held like unwilling statues.

Prospero, in his ducal robes, appeared before them as though risen from the dead.

Antonio and King Alonso were awestruck into true repentance and begged to be forgiven. At last Prospero's anger was placated.

Prospero released them from the circle and led them, and his old friend Gonzalo, to where Ferdinand and Miranda sat playing chess.

King Alonso was overjoyed at finding his son alive and embraced him warmly. Ferdinand told the king of his wish to marry Miranda. Seeing Miranda's beauty and his son's happiness, King Alonso gave his consent. He hoped the union would heal the rift between Milan and Naples.

Into the midst of their rejoicing came Caliban, Trinculo, and Stefano, urged on by Ariel. Prospero forgave them too, in return for a little hard labor. The party then made themselves comfortable, while Prospero recounted his adventures of the past twelve years.

They all planned to sail to Naples the next morning for the wedding of Miranda and Ferdinand, after which Prospero would return to Milan as its rightful duke. That night, Prospero released his faithful Ariel, who promised him fair winds for their journey. Then Prospero discarded his magic cloak, buried his staff deep in the ground, and threw his book of magic out to sea. After twelve years, Prospero was leaving the enchanted island to Caliban and the sprites. Prospero's tempest had served its purpose, and his dukedom was restored.